SORTING

Lynn Peppas

Crabtree Publishing Company
www.crabtreebooks.com

My Path to Math

Author: Lynn Peppas
Coordinating editor: Chester Fisher
Series editor: Penny Dowdy
Editor: Reagan Miller
Proofreader: Ellen Rodger
Editorial director: Kathy Middleton
Production coordinator: Margaret Amy Salter
Prepress technician: Margaret Amy Salter
Cover design: Samara Parent
Logo design: Samantha Crabtree
Project manager: Kumar Kunal (Q2AMEDIA)
Art direction: Dibakar Acharjee (Q2AMEDIA)
Design: Shruti Aggarwal (Q2AMEDIA)
Photo research: Dimple Bhorwal (Q2AMEDIA)

Photographs:
Alamy: image100: front cover (center)
BigStockPhoto: Dabjola: p. 6
Dreamstime: Elnur: p. 17, 18; Guimahky: p. 6, 7; Muhoed: p. 14, 17, 18;
  Shkacas: p. 6, 7
Fotolia: Dana Nicolescu: p. 20, 21; Karen Roach: p. 14, 17, 18; Rozaliya:
  p. 10, 11; Nikola Spasenoski: p. 17, 18; Pamela Uyttendaele: p. 6, 7
Istockphoto: p. 5, 6, 7, 10, 11, 14, 17, 18; Carmen Martínez Banús: p. 8, 23;
  Magdalena Gieniusz: p. 14, 17, 18; Robert Koopmans: p. 4; Anandha
  Krishnan: p. 10, 11; megasquib: front cover (bottom right); Greg
  Nicholas: p. 8, 23; Jan Rihak: p. 14, 17, 18; ZoneCreative: p. 10, 11
Madlen: p. 17, 18
Q2AMedia Art Bank: p. 5, 9, 13, 15, 19
Shutterstock: p. 10, 11, 12, 13; Oleg Avtomonov: p. 16 (left), 17, 18;
  Baloncici: p. 9; Stacy Barnett: p. 20, 21; Katrina Brown: p. 20, 21;
  Deniz Dogan: p. 14, 17, 18; J. Helgason: p. 10, 11; Nataliya Hora:
  p. 20, 21; Andrea Leone: p. 5; Lidian: p. 17, 18; Loskutnikov: p. 1;
  MarFot: p. 10, 11; V. J. Matthew: p. 12; Dmitry Melnikov: p. 16 (right),
  17, 18; Nikolay Okhitin: p. 10, 11; Edyta Pawlowska: p. 10, 11; Elan
  Sablich: p. 6, 7; Roman Sigaev: p. 14, 17, 18; Igor Sokolov: p. 14, 17, 18;
  Sklep Spozywczy: p. 5, 15; Struk Olga: p. 16 (left), 17, 18; Stephanie
  Swartz: p. 10, 11; Tadija: p. 4; Todd Taulman: p. 10, 11

Library and Archives Canada Cataloguing in Publication

Peppas, Lynn
    Sorting / Lynn Peppas.
(My path to math)
Includes index.
ISBN 978-0-7787-4349-1 (bound).--ISBN 978-0-7787-4367-5 (pbk.)

    1. Set theory--Juvenile literature. 2. Similarity judgment--Juvenile
literature. I. Title. II. Series: My path to math

QA248.P46 2009   j511.3'22   C2009-903581-2

Library of Congress Cataloging-in-Publication Data

Peppas, Lynn.
    Sorting / Lynn Peppas.
        p. cm. -- (My path to math)
    Includes index.
    ISBN 978-0-7787-4367-5 (pbk. : alk. paper) -- ISBN 978-0-7787-4349-1
(reinforced lib. bdg. : alk. paper)
    1. Set theory--Juvenile literature. I. Title.

    QA248.P385 2010
    511.3'22--dc22
                                                    2009022915

Crabtree Publishing Company

www.crabtreebooks.com   1-800-387-7650

Published in Canada
Crabtree Publishing
616 Welland Ave.
St. Catharines, ON
L2M 5V6

Published in the United States
Crabtree Publishing
PMB16A
350 Fifth Ave., Suite 3308
New York, NY 10118

Published in the United Kingdom
Crabtree Publishing
Lorna House, Suite 3.03, Lorna Road
Hove, East Sussex, UK
BN3 3EL

Published in Australia
Crabtree Publishing
386 Mt. Alexander Rd.
Ascot Vale (Melbourne)
VIC 3032

Contents

Sorting

Today is Anna's birthday. She gets ready for her party. Anna and her father need to clean the house. Her friends are coming soon! Anna helps **sort** the clean socks and put them away.

You can sort too! Sorting is putting things into **groups**. The things in each group are alike in some way.

▶ These socks are not sorted.

Fact Box

Sorting things that belong together is also called **grouping**.

Sorting is a way of making
groups that belong together.

Alike and Different

Anna sorts the socks by color. She puts white socks in one pile, or group. These socks are **alike**. The socks that are not white do not belong in this group. These socks are **different**.

Things can be alike in many ways. The white socks are alike because they are the same color. Anna could sort another way. Some socks have stripes while others do not.

▼ alike

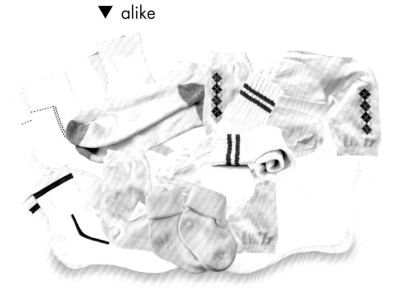

▼ different

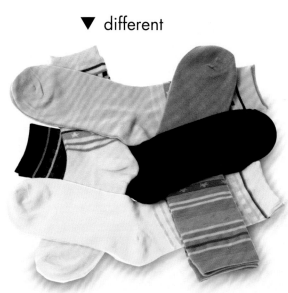

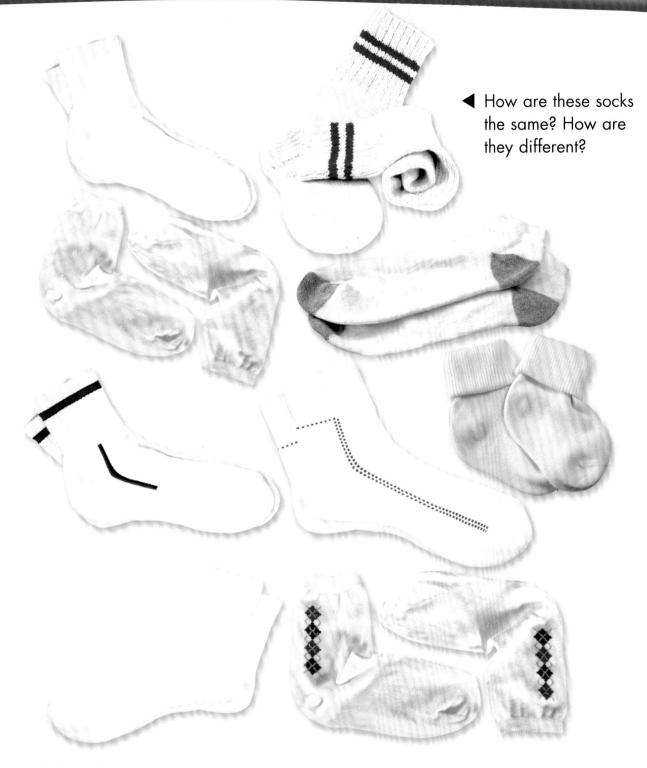

◀ How are these socks the same? How are they different?

Activity Box

Look at the white socks above. Sort them into groups with stripes and without stripes.

We Sort Every Day!

Anna must sort things to **recycle**. We recycle things to use them again. She sorts things by what they are made of. She puts glass in one box. Paper goes in another. Plastic things have their own box. She groups metal together too.

We sort things every day. We sort things to be recycled at home, in schools, and at work.

▼ The color of the recycling box tells us what to sort into each box.

8

Anna can practice sorting as she recycles.

Sorting Rule

Anna can sort things in many different ways. Look at these things for her party. She could sort them by color. She could sort them by what they are made of.

How Anna groups things together is a **sorting rule**. A sorting rule is a way that things can be grouped together. Here, Anna sorted by color. So the sorting rule is color.

◀ What is another sorting rule Anna could use for these objects?

Activity Box

Anna has sorted the things above into two groups. What is her sorting rule?

What does each group above have in common?

Sets

A group of things can be called a **set**. Anna has many dolls. Her dolls make a set. She keeps them together. They belong together because they are all dolls. They have something in common.

One thing in a set is called an **element**. Rachel is Anna's best doll. Rachel is one element of the set of dolls.

element

Activity Box

How many elements do you see in Anna's set of dolls?

Anna's dolls look different from each other. They belong together because they are all dolls.

13

Sorting by Color

Anna's friends come to her party. Each friend brings her a present. Each present is wrapped with a different colored paper. Anna sorts her presents by color. Color is Anna's sorting rule. One color makes one set.

Sorting by color would make many sets because there are many colors. Anna has red, yellow, green, and blue presents. She makes four sets using these colors.

Activity Box

Look at Anna and her friends. How can they be sorted by the color of their clothes?

14

Everything can be sorted by color.

15

Sorting by Size

Anna can sort her presents in other ways too. Anna has some big presents. She has some small presents too. Some of Anna's friends brought gifts that are not big or small. They brought medium–sized presents.

Anna and her friends sort her presents into sets. They use the sorting rule small, medium, and large gifts.

small   medium   large

Count the elements
in each set.

small

medium

large

Activity Box

Which set above has more elements than
the other groups? Which set has the least?

Sorting by Shape

Anna's presents have different shapes. Some presents have straight lines. The sides are flat. The others do not. They have curves. The sides are not flat.

Anna makes a new sorting rule. She sorts her presents by straight lines or curves. The presents with straight lines make a set. Her friend makes a set of presents with curves.

curved lines

straight lines

Activity Box

Count how many sides to these shapes. What is the sorting rule for these sets of pattern blocks?

Which group of pattern blocks has the most elements?

Venn Diagrams

Anna sorts party hats. Using two hula hoops she makes a **Venn diagram**. In a Venn diagram, each circle holds one set. One circle holds the set of yellow hats. The other circle holds the set of blue hats.

Some hats have blue and yellow. The circles cross in the middle. Hats with both colors belong in the middle. They belong in both sets.

Activity Box

Where would this hat go in the Venn diagram?

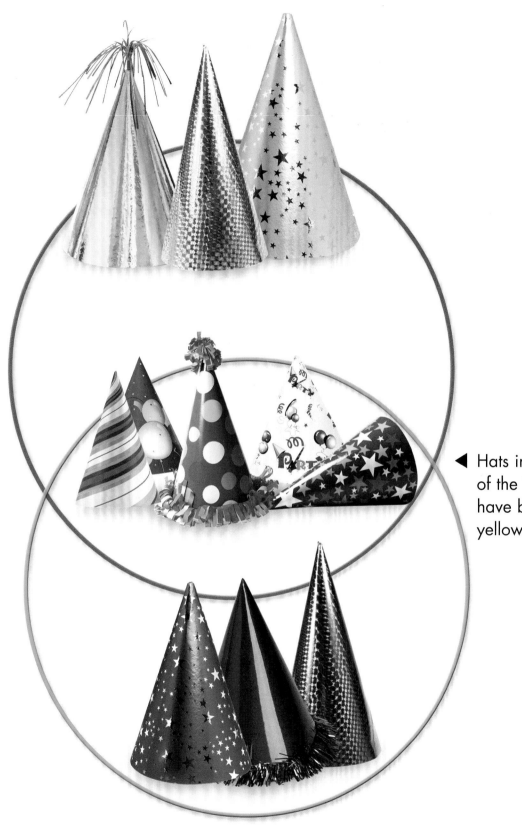

◀ Hats in the middle of the Venn diagram have both blue and yellow in them.

Glossary

alike Two or more things that are the same in some way

different Two or more things that are not the same

element One item or object in a set

group A number of things together

grouping To put things into sets

recycle To use something again so it is not thrown away

set A group of things that belong together

sort To make groups of things that are the same in some way

sorting rule The way in which
items are sorted

Venn diagram Two or more circles that
show how things are alike and different

Index

Printed in the U.S.A. — BG